Chapter 1

It was a dark and damp night in Yodok on the shadow of among the worlds' most reclusive countries. The people, forgotten by even the North Koreans were as isolated as the people could be. The pain and memory of the abused haunted the screams of the mountains as the pain and suffering continued on in the darkness.

The barbed wire fence warped and twisted around Yodok. Violence and abuse were full of pain and suffering as the sadism and abuse engulfed the camp.

This was the regime's most extreme example of sadism that it uses to perpetuate its power, aware that only sadism and propaganda are the two pillars of perpetual motion of the KIm Jong family who rules the land as their personal fiefdom without regard to the 22 million people others.

A land of darkness and shadow for 66 years, untouched by modern convenience, undaunted by the pace of time stood as a monument to the subjugation of the people by the regime.

The mangled wire twisted and contorted across the meadow, the parched brown meadow as the shadow of darkness loomed over the land.

The flag fluttered, blue, white, red and with a star waved in the wind whopping wildly along in the wind.

The totalitarian blocks of buildings stood there in the meadow, stood there abused shattered and memories haunted as the inhabitants were abused and abused over again and again.

The warden began.

"You are a counterrevolutionary, working to defeat the socialist Juche ideology."

"I am just exercising my freedom of speech."

"No you are a traitor."

"No I am not, I am speaking from the heart and I want a better country."

"You are a puppet of American imperialists who wants to overthrow the Democratic Peoples' Republic of Korea."

"No I am not; I am just fighting for the world where the Universal Declaration of Human Rights is respected.'

"That is an American invention."

"No it's not, it's what the United Nations has agreed to."

"If you don't shut up we will rape you and your family."

'You can torture me, kill me and abuse me but you will never silence me, never."

"There have been deaths in Yodok, unfortunate events as they were."

"Yes because the regime does not respect the law."

"What law."

'International human rights and humanitarian law."

"The western intervention? The warden said as he was kicked in the groin."

"Open your mouth you scum and drink my pee."

"AHAHAHAHA."

""Now tell me what are you going to do next?"

"Do what next?"

"You are a traitor."

"I am a traitor, you are committing crimes against humanity."

"You are committing crimes against the Democratic People's Republic of Korea."

"No I am not, I am standing up to my beliefs."

He was kicked in the guts again.

"That's it you are getting reduced rations."

"No I am not, I am standing for my beliefs"

"You are a fraud."

"I am not a fraud."

"You are a threat to the peace and security of the Democratic People's Republic of Korea."

"I am not I am a friend of the Democratic People's Republic of Korea."

"No you are not, you are part of the American imperialists."

"No I am not, I am a Korean through and through."

"I am part of the movement to free the Democratic Peoples' Republic of Korea."

"No you're not."

"I am trying to enforce the Universal Declaration of Human Rights and the Geneva Conventions."

"That's your goal."

"You are insane."

"No I am not."

"Why doesn't North Korea respect international law?"

"We respect all laws including that of the international community."

No you don't you just violate laws with impunity."

"Moi don't."

Another kick in the head with water flowing down with impunity.

Do you want to throw you in the water?

"No but I am standing up and fighting for my beliefs."

"No you are not."

"You are a traitor to the Democratic People's Republic of Korea so is your entire family. You have been imprisoned and you will never get out of here."

You should be happy you are alive.

"I am very happy I am a live but I want to live in a Korea, a unified Korea which respects human rights as enumerated in the Universal Declaration of Human Rights and the Geneva Conventions."

"The Geneva Conventions what the hell are those?"

"The Geneva Conventions are the rules of international humanitarian law, the laws of armed conflict, they tell people how people involved in wartime should be treated there are four such conventions concerning (1) Soldiers (2) Sailors (3) Prisoners of War (4) Civilians.

"So the American imperialists have told North Korea how to behave?"

"No this is what was agreed to by the international community for the last 150 years."

"Really?"

"Why should Korea enforce these laws? Speak before we dump into the river."

"BECAUSE if you talk about developing a modern socialist state you need to respect the rights of the war."

"The rights we respect are the rights of a Juche Socialist Korea."

I like to remind you that Korea has ratified the Geneva Conventions .

"We cannot let the American imperialists dictate policy of Korea."

"Again I remind you this is what the INTERNATIONAL COMMUNITY HAS DECIDED."

"Korea has no place for the international community."

"And what is your name you traitor?"

"My name is Hong Kim Yuk."

"Hong KIm Yuk, I don't know where you got traitors information."

"Kim IISung University where I studied political science."

"HOW the hell did you get into that university?"

"Results, results."

"Yes but you must be able to stand up to your beliefs."

"I will not give up."

"I will stand up for my values."

"You will not leave Yodok."

"Yes I will."

"But we must make North Korea a free democratic country."

"Democracy the American imperialist democracy our democracy is much better than your democracy."

"No democracy is a basic right for all enumerated under the Universal Declaration of Human Rights."

"Another western instrument."

Lee Hong Yuk was kicked in the shins and peed on.

Now pick this up and get to work.

"Get to work."

"Get to work now."

What do you mean I had to get to work now?

"I am fighting for human freedom."

"I am fighting for human freedom."

"You are a traitor."

Now go and clean the feces on the grass.

"Burt I only trying to build a better country."

Yuk Lee Hong, you are the third generation of your family to be in this concentration camp.

Yes and I want the system to end

That's eat no food tonight.

"But I am starving."

"So is the ideology of the Democratic Peoples' Republic of Korea."

The ideology of Democratic Peoples of Korea.

"The ideology of the DPRK is built on tyranny."

That's it no food for two days.

"I bet you have a girlfriend?"

"Yes she lives in Hamhung where I am from."

"How would you like it we find her and we gang rape her?"

"How the fuck do."

"How about your mother and your sister as well?"

You wouldn't

Of course we would and we do it all at once.

"You wouldn't."

Naturally in front of traitors like you.

'You don't know where they are anyway."

"Of Couse we know where they are in Hamhung."

Hong Min-Jim and Hong Jung Hoo.

"Know them?"

"We know where they live."

"And your girlfriend Numi Hyori."

"You wouldn't of course."

"We would?"

I will tell the world about all of this up and to and including the United Nations In New York and Geneva.

"You can't leave the country unless you're from the workers Party. Only they have international passports."

"Well I will sneak across the Yalu into China and expose all of you."

"If you do we will kill you Hung Kim Yuk and your family and your girlfriend."

"Well at least they won't have died in vain."

"That it."

You are a traitor to the Democratic Peoples' Republic of Korea we will kill before the end of next week I alert the executioners. The Total control zone in Yodok cannot hold you.

"You're right it can't."

"And we will station more border guards if you make it to the Yalu which is unlikely Good luck."

"Don't worry I will expose you Goodbye to you."

"Goodbye to you too."

Chapter 2

Lee Hong Yuk slowly wandered through the grass slowly and surely crawling, crawling through the grass through the grass slowly slowly carefully carefully and he was wondering through the barbed wire.

Through the barbed wire without making a single sound.

ZAP ZAP ZAP ZAP

He sunk through the wire.

An alarm bell started but Yuk turned it off slowly and he escaped.

"OK, wow that was close."

"Now I have to walk slowly."

The guard said. "Escape is impossible."

Lee Hong Yuk hid behind a tree.

"Where?"

"I don't know someone escaped. Who was it?"

"I don't know, we must find out."

"Who can it be?"

"We must find out."

"Anyway I don't see anything."

Lee Hong Yuk kept going.

"Good they don't see me maybe 500 more kilometers."

He walked through the meadow slowly.

Carefully carefully

We must persevere

We must persevere

We must preserve

We must persevere

Lee Ong Yuk walked about 5 km.

"We will slowly make it to the Yalu."

"We must smuggle these reports."

Lee Hong Yuk continued to wonder through and through cross the meadow.

Across the meadow

Across the meadow

Across the meadow

The shadow of darkness wondered around the world.

We will prevail

We will prevail

Lee Hong Yuk saw a truck coming.

"Get out."

Lee Hong Yuk walked along the road.

"We will find out the memories."

The memories will haunt me."

"The memories must continue and we will find out the truth."

Lee Hong Yuk escaped.

We will prevail

We will prevail

He slowly walked.

He slowly walked along the meadow.

We will prevail

Lee Hong Yuk walked along the meadow.

Finally he found a house and saw a person.

The person noticed how emaciated he was.

"You look so skinny. What happened? Come in tell me. "

Lee Hong Yuk walked in.

"So what happened?"

"I was in Yodok, do you know that?"

"What's Yodok?"

"It is the largest concentration camp."

"What is a concentration camp?"

"A place where people are held together behind barbed wire."

"So Korea has such camps?"

"Yes, we do."

"So what goes on in these concentration camps?"

"Torture, rape, violence against women, rape slavery, enforced labor."

"Wow"

"Yes, and it must stop."

The bell rang rang.

Ding ding ding dong.

"Who is that?"

"We are from the police "

"We want to know if there are any escapees."

The women responded. "No, I will not contravene Korean law."

"PROVE IT."

"Here is my internal passport with my permit to live here."

"Good, now if there was any escapees from justice you would return them no?"

"Of course, I am a law-abiding citizen."

"Thank you, maam."

Lee Hong Yuk thanked her.

"Thank you beautiful human angel. What is your name?"

"Nun Sung Hyun."

"Awesome."

"GOOD"

"YES"

"Keep going and tell the truth about Korea."

"Thank you Mrs. Nun."

"So where are you going Mr.Yuk?"

"To Geneva."

"That's in Switzerland right?"

"Right."

"Our dear leader went there."

"How are you planning on getting there?"

"I have to smuggle myself across the Yalu into China and then across the Amur into Russia and cross the Trans-Siberian Railroad to Moscow and then onto the train to Berlin and Geneva."

"How are you planning on getting the passports and visa?"

"I need to connect with North Korean expats in China, they can give me documents."

Freedom

Freedom

Freedom

"Thank you for freedom."

"No problem"

"No problem"

"You will bring freedom, human rights and democracy into our country."

Yes in accordance with the Geneva Conventions and the Universal Declaration of Human Rights.

"Yes, keep fighting."

"You will have to leave soon."

"Yes, I know."

"How did you escape from Yodok?"

"Well, I found a weakness in the wire I heard the guards say a week ago that there was a weak spot in the barbed wire 700 meters east of the 5th door. So, I went there."

I can't stand my girlfriends, my family, and people being tortured, raped and physically and mentally abused.

I have a conscience.

Lee Hong Yuk walked across the meadow walked across South Hongyong province marched across slowly and surely across South Hongyong and across the meadow.

Slowly surely

"We will fill found out these people."

"We will find out."

"We will find out."

Slowly surely

"We will find out."

"We will."

"Slowly will find.

'We must find out.

Slowly Lee Hong Yuk meant a police officer.

"Slowly we will invoke freedom."

Freedom freedom

Freedom for all Koreans

In accordance with the Universal Declaration of Human Right.

Freedom

Freedom

Freedom

Freedom

Freedom

Freedom

Enforce the International Covenant on Civil and Political Rights, the International Covenant on Economic, Social and Cultural Rights the Convention on the Rights of the Child.

Convention against Torture

Convention against Racial Discrimination

The Geneva Convention

Enforce international human rights law

Lee Hong Yuk knew that if he was caught treading this police would arrest him.

He put these papers in his folder and onto his jacket.

The police did stop him and say.

"What are you doing?"

"Oh, just walking to my village."

Lee Hong Yuk read the sign.

Kwamjiso

"Are you from Kwanjiso?"

"Yes, I am."

"You know where that is you seem not to be from here?"

"Yes, I am from here."

"What's in your folder?"

"Oh, farming equipment."

"OK, keep farming."

Of course they were major international instruments of international human rights and humanitarian law as defined by the United Nations, Organization of American States, African Union and the European Union.

Freedom

Freedom

Freedom

Freedom

Lee Hong Yik continued speaking the truth about his message.

'We will find the truth about North Korea."

Lee Hong Yuk walked into another province."

From South Hangyong to North Hangyong.

There was immediately a government checkpoint to check people to see if they the proper paperwork to cross borders.

Lee Hong Yuk sneaked past the guard across the mountains.

The guard asked. "Did you hear someone move?"

"Anyone?"

"I thought a saw a person move."

"Well, let's see he can escape."

"I know you are there."

"Open up."

Lee Hong Yuk continued.

He made no sound as he hid across the trees.

Across the meadow

"Ok, he can't escape. We will call the police."

The police showed up.

"So what is going on?"

"There is a person who is violating the terms of his permit."

He crossed from South Hongyong Province to North Hongyong Province without authorization.

"What are we going to do?"

"Well we must scour the area to make sure no intruders get by."

"But what if they do?"

"We return them to where they belong?"

Lee Hong Yuk was scared.

He saw a tiny river and he hid behind there.

"So where do you think he went?"

"I don't know but we must find out."

Lee Hong Yuk continued.

"Well if they do not find them, we will eventually know."

Lee Hong Yuk was terrified.

"Well, we cannot be too far."

"The world must know the truth."

The world must know the truth.

"Where are we going?'

"Over the Yalu River through to China and onto Habra to pick up the Trans Manchurian Railway to Moscow Yarosklavksly Vokzal, across the Circle Line in Moscow, to Belarussiki Vokzal, then the train to Berlin, then the train to Zurich, and Geneva

Lee Hong Yuk continued through North Hongyong Province.

He stayed at another place.

"Hello, my name is Nam Song Jim."

"Yes, you are vesting, are you?"

"Yes, I got my permit here."

"Good, come in"

"So, tell me where are you going?"

"Well, I am just vesting family in the edge of the North Hongyong Province."

"Ok"

There was a knock on the door.

"Hello, police open up."

"Yes, police?"

"We have news that there is a counter revolutionary in your house. "

Nun Son-Jgin responded. "I had no idea."

"Yes, well, now you do."

"Yes, I will certainly cooperate with the authorities."

Lee Hong Yuk took out a bathroom plunger and smashed the window open and left.

There was a crashing sound and Lee Hong Yuk muttered to himself. "If they know…"

Of course, he spent the next four days hiding in trees and brunches as he approached the Yalu, the natural border between North Korea and China.

"The hardest border crossing yet."

I know there are expats in Harbin who can provide me with false passport and visa to cross the Russian, Belarusian and Schengen Zone boundaries but it's up to me to cross into China.

I will prepare for midnight, Midnight on the Yalu.

There was barbed wire guards every 500 meters across the 350 kilometer border so 700 guards in all, police severe checkpoints mines everything.

"This is the worst border I have to devise a plan to get across into China myself.

I have Korean defector friends in Harbin, the capital of Heilongjiang province, they can provide fake documents and visa across Russian, Belarusian, and Schegen Zone borders but I must cross the Yalu myself.

Let's see it been 20 days since I left Yodok I walked the 200 kilometers from Yodok, I am so skinny, I hope they give me good meals once I get to Harbin. I don't know how much renminbi I have to get to Harbin.

OK, I will come to a conclusion but first I must escape North Korea.

Chapter 3

So the spic crossing of the Yalu began.

Swimming against the current, against the guard 3 kilometers across 3 kilometers across the longest three kilometers of his life.

Guards every 700 meters on the 350 kilometer border between North Korea and China barbed wire along the border, watching with infrared cameras spying on the person.

"Look at that! We have an escapee!"

The person responded in Chinese and Korean. "Renmin tao Chaoxian."

Person escaping from North Korea.

Bullets fired bullets raged.

Bullets raged over and over again.

Fire destruction.

Destruction

Bullets

Violence

Devastation

I SEE YOU

THERE HE IS

A bullet missed Lee Hong Yuk by 200 meters, the next one even closer by 50 meters IT was only 800 meters swim across the river, 2200 meters to go.

900 meters more bullets.

1000 meters, one kilometer dogs.

Gou Gou Gou Gou

There stood the bridge along the road to China.

1500 meters, halfway through and the cascade of bullets from both started.

"Chaxoin Renmin miao."

Lee Hong Yuk understood enough Chinese from his Korean expats to know what was going on.

Violence

Violence

Violence

"I must make to freedom."

"I will make it."

2500 meters and the current whipped him.

I must make it

I must make it

He crossed into the Chinese side on the Heilongjiang province and was immediately arrested by the Chinese Peoples Armed Police, Zhonggua Renmin WUzhang Jingcha Buida.

"What is you name?"

"Lee Hong Yuk."

"Why have you illegally violated Chinese territorial integrity?"

"I lost my passport."

"What are you really doing?"

"Gong you renquan Chaxoian."

"Renquan?"

"Shiju Renquan Xuanyuan."

"Shiyue Shi yiwan jiuwan sishiba."

"Guojirenquantian"

"Wo Shuo Zhongwen?"

"Ne sheng Zhognwen penggyou Chaoxian min Zhonggua."

"Wo Shuo Zhonghua Zhongwen."

OK the fact that you can speak Chinese that well does not dissuade the fact that your crossed the border illegally.

"Well I crossed the border ultimately to go overload to Switzerland to the UN Human Rights Council in Geneva."

"You are not afraid?"

"Why would I be, you can detain me, torture me, even kill me but I WILL BE HEARD."

"I WILL BE HEARD."

"Yes, fine. I could detain you but you like you said if you can slip out of North Korea you can slip out of jails so there is no point."

Here's the deal you have 15 days to leave China and go back to North Korea or we will deport you.

We have your name we know where you are and we can find you.

"If in the most unlikely circumstance you make it to Switzerland, which I sincerely doubt if you mention the treatment of North Koreans in China you will be denied future visas to China, even on a Swiss passport.

"Fine", said Lee Hong Yuk.

The officer from Zhonggua. "Renmin Wuchang Buda."

"Ok, 15 days or we find and deport you."

Lee Hong Yuk politely said. "I will find the closest train station and take the train back to Pyongyang, the capital."

"Good, zaijuan then."

"Zaijuan."

Of course Lee Hong Yuk had no intention of going back to North Korea.

He was going to hitchike to Harbin to find Korean friends there.

He found a black market store when he decided to change North Korean won to renminbi.

"Wo yao wuwan renminbi."

"OK"

He got his five thousand renminbi and begins asking for a trip to Harbin.

He decided to hitchike and found a new person.

"Wo yao Luxing Harbin?"

"OK, siwan renminbi."

The person followed the road to Habra and three hours later arrived in the city.

Lee Hong Yuk responded. "Shay Shay."

He screamed.

Chozuche

Chozuche

Chozuche

Finally after 20 minutes a taxi came and said. "Hangguo Faguan Harbin."

The taxi driver came to a Korean restaurant in the middle of Harbin on Nanji Street.

Lee Hong Yuk walked in. "Ni Hao Ming Xing Zi Lee Hong Yuk Min Chaoxianren."

"Ok, you can talk to the owner he came help you."

The owner came and responded in Korean. "I can provide you shelter?"

"Are you trying to resettle in South Korea?"

"No, I want to report the situation to the UN human council in Switzerland."

"So you are traveling to Switzerland how?"

"Overland through North Korea, China, Russia, Belarus, Poland, Germany and Switzerland."

"That's a long trip."

"Yes, and I need help from the Korean expat/defector community in these countries."

"Yes, yes yes I have friends in Moscow who can help you with Russian visas, Belarusian transit visa, and the Schengen Visa."

"How I am going to get a passport first?"

"There is a store Jihong Street it makes photographs and I can sell you a Korean passport for 100 renminbi."

"Ok."

Lee Hong Yuk dutifully obeyed got the passport photos and paid the 100 renminbi and got the passport.

"I will also need Russian visa, Russian rubles and knowledge of the Russian language as I make it to Moscow."

"All of which can be provided by my Korean friends in Moscow."

"I will call them."

He called them in a four hour time zone difference.

7 495 3243549

"Zdrative eta tva drug v harbin, kitana."

"Zdratsvie zaushmi ti zvenshi?"

"Novi defector ot Severenya Korea."

"Ah, oh hush dengi, visa y russiki yzik da?"

"Da."

"Oh hush zhenit vi russi?"

"Net, oh idut soviet prava chelovka organzasie obedniya nasie v svitseria."

"Cherez Rusia?"

'Rusia, Belarusia, schengenzski zona."

"Ya pomogov vis y dengi."

"Mishit bit 70,000 ruble y visa."

"Da"

"Spas Ibo."

He spent the next day in Harbin and went to get the taxi.

Chozuche

Chozuche

The taxi showed up.

"Houche zhan."

Twenty minutes he arrived to the train station in central Harbin.

He said. "Piao Mosike."

Lee Hong Yuk gave his fake passport hoping the attendant would not notice.

He seemed oblivious to everything.

"Houche Mosike houche jiu feizhong."

"Shay Shay."

The train arrived at 9 and Lee Hong Yuk left China with 8 days to spare.

"Four hours, si feizhong and I am at the Russian border."

Ch
apter 4

The train left the gray industrial mess of Harbin passing through the Sikhote Alin Mountrains of northeastern Heilongjiang province, four hours across the province, one of China's largest provinces and slowly and surely the train arrived on the Russian border, along the river, the Heilongjiang river in China, the Amur river in Russia.

Lee Hong Yuk breathed a breath.

"Let's hope this deception game pays off."

Thank god for my friends who gave me this Russian phrase book.

"Passport pazuluista."

Lee Hong Yuk took out his fake South Korean passport.

The officer looked at him and said nothing.

He seemed suspicious.

He began talking very slowly in Russian, seeing that his physical appearance, did not endear him to be of Russian descent.

"Til out Yuzhny Korea?"

"Da."

"Da ya yadun v Moskvee looking at his phrasebook."

The guard looked at him.

"Eta tvu ochbnik?"

Lee Hong Yuk said "da".

"Ti ushih russiki izik?" again the guard said slowly.

"Da."

"Ti hushu znet v rossiya?"

Lee Hong Yuk said. "Net, ya yen v svitseria va conferencia organzasie obedenniya nasie."

"Na pozedit? It budush preskit v Moskvie pravinia?"

"Da."

"Hurush na sprasi eti voprozoev potumusha next koreansit tow zevit rossiya illegalnya."

Lee Hong Yuk took a deep sigh of relief.

He had beaten the second country's borders.

The train crossed the Heilongjiang/Amur rivers into the Russian Federation and into the Amur Oblast.

Lee Hong Yk relaxed he was going to be on this train for a few days and he decided he only lived once and decided to try some vodka.

He took out some of his rubles and drank vodka.

"Well, I lied across two international boundaries, two to go, halfway."

He decided to take a drink of some more vodka and he saw a couple of people playing chess.

He jumped in of course.

Of course, he slowly managed to mate the queen and win two games and he thought. "Well, this is how my life, slowly and beautifully I will win, I will win."

Three hours later the train left Amur Oblast and entered Zaybakalsky Krai and he passed across Lake Baikal, the deepest lake in the world. "Well, another five days to go."

Let's see how far we can build the case.

Lee Hong Yuk began to prepare his documents, the Universal Declaration of Human Rights, the International Covenant on Civil and Political Rights, the International Covenant on Economic, Social, and Cultural Rights, the Convention on the Rights of the Child, the Convention on the Elimination of all Forms of Discrimination against Women, and the other conventions.

As the train continued into Buryatia Lee Hong Yuk continued proudly.

"I will bring human rights and democracy to my country I will."

he began to speak in Russian from the phrasebook using horrible grammar with a friend he met Sergei.

"Sergei otkuda ti?"

"Ah, ya et Perm."

"Okuda ti it somutish kak ti et Korea deta."

"Da Severnye Korea."

"Ah, ti robohsnit?"

"'Het, ya yedu svitseria robota na prava chelovka v Geneva."

"Ah."

"Da."

"Shtua eta?"

"Raziny konvensie na prava chelvaka organzasie obednniya nasie."

"Ani roboti v Geneva?"

"Da."

"Tva russiki horoshi."

"Ya roboti na slovar."

The train stopped in Irkutsk for the night in the administrative center of Irkutsk Oblast.

CHAPTER

5

Lee Hong Yuk left Irkutsk at midnight heading westward to Moscow across Siberia on the continuation of the Trans-Siberian Railway, the Trans Sibersky Magisterial in Russian and onto the Krasnoyarsk krait and the city of Krasnoyarsk a city of nearly a million people the train kept rumbling on and onward.

He began to practice his Chinese with the Chinese passengers on board some of whom had boarded in Beijing and Shenyang further south than Harbin.

"Ni Hao ming xing xe Lee Hong Yuk Ni Min Chaoxian."

"NI Min Wen Ping Min Shenyang Jilinsheng, jing Jilin Sheng."

"Ni min yiniminzhe eloshi ni gong Mosike."

"Yinminzihe eloshi Lee Hong Yuk?"

"La, ni gong renquan Chaoxican ne luxing Rinewa, Rishi wao Lianhegguo."

"Ming."

Another Russian passenger came with a souvenir and began to speak.

"Ni sheng Zhonggua La sheng Zhonggua ming."

Lee Hong Yuk responded in Russian. "Ya zenyu no ya ne razgovinia pa russiki horosoha."

"Ti olushi russiki izik pravinya y vizhi slovar."

"Ya zenuiyu?"

"Da, oloshni horosho."

The train continued into the city of Krasnoyarsk. There he stood five thousand kilometers from home.

Beautiful

Beautiful

The wilds of Siberia continued.

The steppes the forest and the wilds.

Russia is the worlds' most forest country Lee Hong Yuk reminded himself 40 percent of the country is forested.

He continued through onto Khakassia and then through Kemerovo Oblast.

Freedom

Freedom

Freedom for all our people

Freedom for our people

He muttered to himself as he walked across the wilderness the forest beautiful wilderness.

Steppes

Steppes and forests

Forest and freedom

Leaving Kemerovo Oblast and onto Novosibirsk and Novosibirsk Oblast the third largest city in Russia.

Seeing the city approach gave Lee Hong Yuk a new sense of freedom.

We are building a society based on freedom.

Based on freedom for all humanity.

For all humanity beautiful precious freedom.

We must win.

Lee Hong Yuk continued on to freedom.

"We must bring human rights to North Korea."

"Enforce the Universal Declaration of Human Rights."

Freedom

Freedom

Slowly we will bring freedom and justice.

The battle continued stronger and stronger.

Freedom

Freedom

The train continued into Omsk Oblast and onto the city of Omsk.

"Another step closer to Geneva."

"Another stop to Geneva."

"We must enforce the human rights regime."

"We must enforce the Universal Declaration of Human Rights, the International Covenant on Civil and Political rights, and the International Covenant on Economic, Social and Cultural Rights."

Freedom

Freedom

No more concentration camps, no more rape, no more torture, no more executions.

No more gulags, freedom of speech, freedom of assembly.

Freedom

Freedom

Slowly and surely the train left Omsk and into Tyumen Oblast.

Another trip continued.

Slowly we will leave Siberia and head into the populated parts of Russia.

Freedom

Freedom

Slowly and surely freedom

Freedom

Freedom

I cannot believe our luck. We are almost home.

He met another Chinese person on the train and began communicating with him.

"NI hao Ming xing xee Lee Hong Yuk. Hangguoren."

"Ah, min chengsha?"

"Busan" Lee Hong yuk lied as that was the location of his fake passport.

"NI Zhongguaren. chengsha Shanghai Ni luxing ROndon houche."

kaisu houche Shanghai Beijing
houche Beijing Moscow
houche Moscow Pariya
kaisu houche Parya Rondon

"Ya Da Luxing?"

"Min luxing?"

"Rinewa."

The train continued through Tyumen Oblast and into Sverdlovsk Oblast into Yekaterinburg the last major city in Asian Russia.

"Goodbye Asia and hello Europe."

The train began the climb over the Ural Mountains.

Slowly we will come to our senses.

Freedom

Freedom

Freedom for all

The train stopped in Yekaterinburg for the night.

"We will bring human rights, freedom and justice to North Korea."

Chapter 6

Lee Hong Yuk left Yekaterinburg getting closer and closer to Moscow.

"A major stop of my travels is coming soon."

The train continued past Sverdlovsk Oblast and into the Perm Krai.

The scenery dramatically changed as the train started to climb the Ural Mountains and into Europe.

"Bye bye Asia, it was nice knowing you," Lee Hong Yuk said.

He decided to play another game of chess with the chess partners.

However, unexpectedly the Russian border police came in.

"Passport, pazuluista."

Lee Hing Yuk came in.

"Yes?" Lee Hong Yuk gave his fake South Korean passport.

"Zdratsvuite."

"Zdratsive, ti ot uzhniy Korea?"

"Da."

"Ti yedizhy v Mosckvi."

"Da."

"Zdrovna"

"Horosho"

The train left Perm Krai and entered Kirov Oblast as the train entered into Europe.

"Slowlty and surely."

"We will prevail"

"We will prevail"

"Freedom"

"Freedom"

Slowly and surely we will achieve our goals.

"Freedom for human rights in North Korea in accordance with the Universal Declaration of Human Rights, the International Covenant on Cave and political Rights, international Covenant on economic Social and Cultural rights."

"Freedom"

"Freedom"

"Freedom"

The Ural Mountains continued but slowly became smaller and smaller as the train.

The train left Kirov Oblast and into Kostroma Oblast.

"Slowly and surely we will bring freedom to North Korea."

"Freedom"

The train continued through the Kirov Oblast several kilometers continued through the oblast into Yaroslavl Oblast and eh saw some people discussing a political meeting.

He spoke in his rusty Russian

Kak dela?"

"Shti ti delish?"

"Mn podgorvika na meeting v Moskvee Mbl chasti spravidniya russia

"Stou eta?"

"Leviya politichisnki parti"

Lee Hong Yuk continued

"Ya robotonu na prava chelovka ti znakomish na prava chelovka?"

'Zaknomin Vcevashinya Decklarasi prava chelovka vce 30 prav."

"Da"

"Da"

Very rapidly they approached the train station in Yaroslavl and they continued to talk.

"Tii yedishu moskve?"

"Net ya yednv v Switzerria?"

"Ah?"

"Da Organzasie Obednenniya Natsie soviet na prava chelovka?"

"Da"

"Til znakomish na vce Mexnaarodiny bill prava chelovka?"

'Da, Vcevashniya Deklarasie Prava Chelovka, Mexnarodinny Pact gradunski y politishiki prav, mexnarodny pact ekonomieskhi y socialiny y cultrany prav."

"Da"

Eventually the train left Yaroslavl and the Oblast and entered Vladimir Oblast.

He finally found a person he could speak to in Korean.

"Hello, my name is Lee Hong Yuk."

"Sit down, you are also traveling to Moscow right?"

"Yes I am."

"What are you doing there?"

'You want to hear a lie or the truth?"

"The truth."

"OK, I am escaping a concentration camp in North Korea which practices rape, torture, and executions."

"Wow!"

"I in fact do have friends, Korean friends, and North Korean defectors in Moscow they run a small Korean restaurant near the third circle road you get off the Leninsky Prospekt metro station."

"Good, what line is that?"

"Schabarkslokya Pokravatska."

"You take the circle line koltsevya to Prospekt Mira and hop on that line to Lenninsky Propsekt."

"They can rent you a room and give you fake transit visa for Belaarus and a fake Schengen visa for Poland, Germany and Switzerland."

"Thank you so much."

The train left Vladimir Oblast and into Moscow Oblast, podmoskovy in Russian.

"Almost home."

"Almost home."

"We are going to the restaurant and spending a night in Moscow."

"Afterwards we are going to get our visa for Belarus."

Slowly the forests disappeared and the buildings started to increase.

Started to increase and eventually Lee Hong Yuk came into Yaroslavklsy vokzal.

"Well, welcome to Moscow."

"I did it the longest train journey yet."

"I just have to find the Korean restaurant."

He decided to take the Circle Line of Moscow to Kaluzhnsyki Kazunshikya aat the Oktrybskyaya station and onto lennisky propsekt on the Kauluzhesyki Kazunshikaya line.

He walked to the Korean restaurant and spoke clearly in Korean.

"I have escaped from a concentration camp in North Korea and I am traveling to Switzerland overland."

"Awesome, we can arrange a visa and staying tonight."

"We will give 5,000 euros to make it to Switzerland a Belarusian transit visa."

"Thank you."

"No problem."

They walked along Lennsinky Prospekt to their tiny apartment."

"Good night."

"Good night."

Chapter 7

Lee Hong Yuk was sleeping in the tiny Moscow apartment. Tiny rooms, tiny corridors.

'Well, I guess real estate is expensive here.

"What can I do?"

He woke up at 7 am and there were his Korean friends.

He began to communicate with them.

"oO you still have my Belarusian and Schengen Visas?"

"Yes, we do."

"Awesome."

"You will expose crimes against humanity and war crimes in North Korea in Geneva?"

"Of course I will."

"So why did you decided to travel overland and not by plane?"

"Well, two reasons. One is that I don't have the money for a plane ticket and two even if I did it would be very very suspicious."

"Yes, I know."

"We got your Belarusian transit visas, awesome."

"I hope you can have a good time but first let's have some breakfast, some porridge?"

"I will."

"So, how do you like Moscow?"

"It is ok I guess not much to say."

"Well, you can continue the good fight here."

"Yes, I must certainly will."

He left the apartment infused with cash in Moscow and headed back to Belarussky Vokzal in on the circle Line and brought two tickets to Berlin.

"Dva billet Berlini."

"Passport y visa pazulsta?"

"Toot."

"Spasibo, billet stoit 12000 rubles."

Lee Hong Yuk gave 12,000 rubles out of his 50,0000.

"Here you go."

He eventually boarded the train leaving Moscow and heading through to the Belarusian border.

He left the city of Moscow passing by the city's famous ring road and left Moscow Oblast eventually and heading through Smolensk Oblast.

"Ok in a few short hours I will be in Belarus."

The ticket collector caught his ticket."

"Berlin eto krasivi gorod."

"Spasibo."

"Spasibo."

He arrived at the Belarusian border determined to illegally enter his third country.

"Passport pazulsta?"

"Toot."

The Belarusian authorities spoke clearly. "Hello Lee Hong Yuk it is a surprise to see a Korean so far in Belarus where are you going?"

"I am going to Switzerland y induct v Svitseria."

"Ok, what for?"

"I have a meeting there."

"OK, your transit visa seems in order good luck."

The train continued into Belarus and in a few hours he arrived in Minsk.

"Slowly and surely there was a member of the Korean community in Minskto give him documents> he began to talk in Russian."

"Svoboda na vce Koreansitz."

"Svoboda"

"Svoboda"

"Dokument, visa, y dengi 5,000 euros."

"Spasibo"

"Spasibo"

He left Belarus energized and determined to get freedom for his people.

"Freedom"

"Freedom"

He took out a copy of the Universal Declaration of Human Rights and began to read Article 28:

- Everyone is entitled to a social and international order in which the rights and freedoms set forth in this Declaration can be fully realized.

And we will fulfill.

'We will fulfil.

The train continued through the fields and forests of Belarus.

"Freedom"

"Freedom"

"Freedom"

"Freedom"

"We will prevail"

"We will prevail"

"Freedom"

"Freedom"

"We will prevail"

"Slowly and surely we will come to an end."

"We will be free again."

We will open the concentration camps.

We will open up so people can see.

'We will bring freedom."

"Freedom"

"Freedom"

In another two hours Lee Hong Yuk arrived at the external border of the European Union and the Schengen Zone along the Belarusian/Polish border.

"Freedom, Freedom."

CHAPTER

8

Lee Hong Yuk prepared for his entry to the Schengen Zone along one of its external borders. The last border to cross.

"Let's see if it works."

The guy spoke in French and English the two most commonly spoken languages in the European Union.

"Passportes, please."

"Passportes, sil vous plait."

Lee Hong Yuk got out his passport.

The officer spoke usually most sign language.

"You are sure that this is the correct passport?"

'Yes" Lee Hong Yuk said without hesitating.

"Well, looks legitimate, welcome to the European Union."

He continued into Poland along the train.

The guy came to him and spoke in Chinese.

"Ni luxing?"

'Luxing Rinewa."

"Oh, wow!"

"Hangguoren?"

"Ni hangguoren."

"Na."

"Min luxing?"

"Rinewa, rishi."

"Luxing?"

"Na, Ne gong renquan lianhegguo renquan weiyuan."

The train continued through the Polish meadows and fields.

Corn fields maize fields abounded from the train window.

Slowly the train crossed over the VIstula river and into Warsaw.

The beautiful 15th century downtown of Warsaw stood resplendent in the shadow of the Vistula.

"Beautiful."

"beautiful."

"Beautiful."

Freedom freedom freedom

The train left Warsaw heading across the A2 Autostrada heading west to Krakow.

Lee Hong Yuk was thinking.

"Getting closer and closer to my destination."

Freedom

Freedom

To enforce the Universal Declaration of Human Rights, the International Covenant on Civil and Political Rights, the International Covenant on Economic, Social and Cultural rights.

Freedom

Freedom

Freedom

Slowly the train arrived at the beginning of Germany.

The conductor said in Polish and English.

90 kilometers to Berlin.

'That's where I will change trains to Zurich."

Chapter 9

The train crossed into Germany and within an hour Lee Hong Yuk entered the German capital, Berlin.

He saw three train schedules to Zurich and saw that the next train was in 5 hours.

He decided to explore Berlin for a while.

"The old Berlin Wall, the Brandenburg Gate, and all the sights of the parks of the Spree."

Freedom

Freedom

This is the kind of freedom I wished I had in North Korea.

If it had freedom, things will become different.

It will be different.

He stood up eating a Berliner donut.

Deliciosu

Delicious

Delicious

Freedom and wonderful freedom

Freedom

Freedom

The Universal Declaration of Human Rights, the Convention on the Rights of the Child, Convention on the Elimination of all Forms of Discrimination against Women.

Freedom

Freedom

Freedom

He followed the old Berlin Wall.

The memory of the wall continued.

Continued across the shadow.

:That's where the old wall stood.

That's what needs to be done.

This is what needs to be done.

Freedom

Freedom

The skyscrapers stood very tall.

Freedom from torture.

Freedom from rape.

Freedom from executions.

Freedom

Freedom must be increased freedom for all.

Freedom for all.

Slowly three hours passed by.

The freedom of Lee Hong Yuk made his life feel so much better.

After all of these years in a concentration camp I can finally be myself.

Freedom for all.

Freedom for all.

Freedom for all.

Lee Hong Yuk left Berlin on the Intercity Express from Berlin to Zurich.

"I will be in Zurich in five hours."

How amazing.

He managed to buy a French book for his stray in Geneva.

"It will be very very useful." thought Lee Hong Yuk.

He began practicing.

"Food comes."

"Drink babe."

Train train

My name eis J M Appel

Freedom

Freedom

We will bring freedom.

No more abuse no more abuse.

Freedom

Freedom

We will stand tall.

Beautiful beautiful

Freedom Freedom

He begin to see the soaring Alps as the train entered the German state of Bavaria.

These soaring mountains are beautiful.

Lee Hong Yuk continued into the state of Baden Wurtttemberg and onto the Swiss frontier.

Switzerland, being a member of the Schengen Zone did not require border controls but since it was not a member of the European Union it still required immigration and regulation checks.

Of course they quickly figured out or at least they though that Lee Hong Yuks passport was legitimate so they let him pass.

"FINALLY SWITZERLAND"

He smiled and said "Here I am".

Chapter 10

As the train entered Switzerland Lee Hong Yuk emerged unscathed.

"Freedom! I did it, I escaped from North Korea into Switzerland."

"I just hope I can tell my story at the UN human rights council in Geneva."

"I just have to work on my French, well that would be the fourth language I studied, after Korean, Chinese, Russian and French."

Freedom Freedom

The majestic blue mountains of Switzerland sparkled brilliantly and the reflection stood up to the world.

"We are going to find out who is responsible for violations of the Universal Declaration of Human Rights, The International Covenant on Civil and Political Rights, The International Covenant on Economic, Social and Cultural Rights, the Convention on the Rights of the Child, The Convention on the Elimination of all Forms of Discrimination against Women, the Geneva Conventions."

Freedom

Freedom

Freedom

Freedom

We are going to speak out for human rights sin North Korea.

Freedom

The train arrived in Zurich Haptbahnhof the main train station in Zurich.

"We are going to go there."

"We are going to get there."

He asked in French. "Je me voudraime billet ent Geneve."

"Ok", the guy said and he only spoke German, the language of the Zurich canton.

"Here you go 150 Swiss Francs."

"Wow, that expensive."

"It's the price."

"Well, I guess I have no choice."

Lee Hong Yuk took the train to Geneva a four hour trip.

"We shall be home soon."

"Home soon.'

"I see If I can find a hotel and everything."

The train passed majestic lakes and mountains forests and glaciers.

"What a beautiful country."

"What a beautiful gorgeous country."

"Freedom for all of humanity."

The train continued through the mountains and Alps of Switzerland.

Three hundred kilometers from Zurich to Geneva were to be covered.

"We will prevail."

"We will overcome."

Lee Hong Yuk spoke clearly in broken French.

"Je me appel Lee Hong Yuk je me Corea du Nord."

They asked why he was in Switzerland.

Travai pour droits d l'homme en Corea Du Nord."

"Wow!"

"Wow!"

Mountains and forest continued vast lakes vast snowy lakes freedom.

Freedom

Freedom

"We will prevail and we will put and to human rights violations."

The train continued.

Freedom

Freedom

The train eventually entered Geneva.

"FINALLY I am home."

He went to a cheap hostel in Geneva, cheap for Switzerland's standards at any rate 36 Swiss Francs."

The Geneva Youth Hostel stood in a nondescript part of town and he liked it that way.

"Quiet, peaceful."

He said," "Tomorrow we will give the United Nations hell" and fell asleep.

CHAPTER
11

Lee Hong Yuk woke up on a bright summer Swiss day ready to go to the UN Human Rights Council.

"We will prepare them for the night."

He took the trip down the trip down the 15 bus (quinze en Francais).

Slowly we can achieve our goals.

Slowly we can achieve our goals.

We can fulfil our dreams.

We will overcome.

40 minutes he stood in front of the Palace of Nations, Palais de Nations in French.

"He spoke Liberte pour alle."

"Liberte pour alle."

"Liberte pour alle."

"Liberte pour alle."

The person responded. "Qual est problem?"

"Je me quere a parler con probleme de droits l'homme en Coree de Nord."

"OK, tene qualifications?"

"Oui est escapee de camp concetracion."

"Wow!"

"OK le program intialise en deux oure."

"Merci beaucoup."

He entered the Palace of Nations.

He went through security and got a victors pass.

Awesome

Awesome

Freedom

Freedom

He slowly achieved his goals.

Freedom

Freedom

He was going to enforce the Universal Declaration of Human Rights and the Convention on the rights of the child.

Freedom

Freedom

Freedom

We can achieve we want.

He began his report and began to speak louder and louder.

"The North Korean government regularly uses torture, rape, execution, punishments she death penalty to abuse and manipulate people."

"It uses concentration camps."

"It abuses human rights left and right."

"It violates all 30 articles of the Universal Declaration of Human Rights it violates the International Covenant on Civil and Political Rights, the International Covenant on Economic, Social and Cultural Rights."

Freedom

Freedom

"That' what 22 million North Koreans want."

"Freedom to enforce the Universal Declaration of Human Rights, the Convention on Rights of the Child, The Geneva Conventions."

"Freedom for all of people."

"No more torture."

"No more genocide."

"No more crimes against humanity."

"Freedom for everyone."

"Freedom for all 22 million North Koreans."

"Freedom for all of humanity."

"Then he switched to French."

"Je me travai pour les droits d l' Homme fi Corea De Nord."

"Respecte les conventions Geneve, les conventions droits d'l enfant Responsibilite pour Protégé."

"Liberte pour alle humanin."

"Liberte pour alle humanin."

The speakers in the Palais de Nations gave him a standing ovation.

"You are incredible!"

"You are amazing!"

"We are going to put an end to these abuses."

Lee Hong Yuk continued. "I have traveled across seven countries.

North Korea

China

Russia

Belarus

Poland

Germany

Switzerland

We will prevail

Freedom for all of humanity

We will prevail

We will prevail

We will find out and punish the person responsible

Yes we will."

Then Lee Hong Yuk clearly pokes.

Freedom

Freedom

CHAPTER
12

The fight continued as the people responsible came forward.

Freedom

Freedom

Freedom

We will prevail

We will prevail

Freedom

The people were brought to Geneva exposing the truth.

"We will win and we will enforce the Universal Declaration of Human Rights and we will enforce the Convention on the Rights of the Child, and we will enforce the Geneva Conventions."

We will prevail

The people were brought before the Palais de Nations.

Freedom

Freedom

We will bring the people to justice.

The group arrived at the meeting and they began to discuss how they were not in charge of the abuses.

Lee Hong Yuk clarified differently.

"You are charged with abuse and we found you."

"We have found you."

"We will punish you."

"We will not be abused."

"We will be free."

Freedom for the abused.

Freedom for the abused .

Freedom

"Beautiful precious freedom."

The people stood in front of the people.

The head of the center Poul Cartier spoke in French.
"Les situation en Corea du Nord est tries horrible Les violation de loi international humanitaire le violations de droits d l'homme que ecrite en Convention Geneve."

Liberte pour alle

Liberte pour alle

Liberte pour alle

Freedom

The argument continued incessantly.

"We didn't do it."

Lee Hong Yuk spent more corroborative evidence.

"Torture, rape, execution, political persecutions, starvation, abuse."

"Abuse that constitutes crimes against humanity under Article 7 of the Rome Statute of International Criminal Court ."

They must be prosecuted.

They must be set an example.

No more genocide, war crimes, and crimes against humanity.

No more abuse.

No more abuse.

No more abuse.

Lee Hong Yuk continued to the International Criminal Court.

"We will prosecute them in accordance with Articles 5, 6, 7, 8 of e Rome Statute."

Freedom for all our people.

Freedom and democracy.

Freedom and democracy.

Freedom and democracy, no more violations of the Geneva Conventions or the Rome Statute.

Freedom and democracy.

"We will respect the Universal Declaration of Human Rights we will respect the International Covenant on Civil and Political Rights, the International Covenant on Economic, Social and Cultural Rights we will respect international human rights and humanitarian law."

We will prevent these abuses.

We will stop them.

Lee Hong Yuk testified in front of the International Criminal Court in front of chief prosecutor Fatou Bensouda.

"The people united shall never be defeated. Weill not be defeated."

Freedom Freedom for all of humanity.

The prosecutor continued to speak.

The situation in North Korea is very grave and it violates International human rights and humanitarian law.

The Geneva Conventions must be respected.

The Hague Conventions must be respected as well.

The Rome Statute must be enforced.

Freedom

Freedom

The verdict was swift and stunning.

They were all sentenced to life imprisonment in Norway.

Freedom

Freedom

Freedom

www.ingramcontent.com/pod-product-compliance
Lightning Source LLC
Chambersburg PA
CBHW060642290526
45793CB00001B/362